Contents

Nature's Children

WHALES

Mark Shawver

Grolier

FACTS IN BRIEF

Classification of common North American whales
Class: *Mammalia* (mammals)
Order: *Cetacea* (whales, dolphins and porpoises)
Suborder: *Mysticeti* (baleen whales);
            Odontoceti (toothed whales)
Genus: Species that frequent North American waters fall into 9 genera.
Species: 12 species of whales and dolphins are commonly found in the oceans around North America.

World distribution.   Varies with species.

Habitat.   Both coastal waters and open ocean.

Distinctive physical characteristics.   Flippers and tail flukes; blowhole, air passage, on top of head; body is covered and streamlined by a layer of blubber.

Habits.   Vary with species.

Diet.   Toothed whales: fish, squid and marine mammals; baleen whales: plankton.

Published originally as
"Getting to Know . . . Nature's Children."

This series is approved and recommended by the Federation of Ontario Naturalists.

Canadian Cataloguing in Publication Data

Shawver, Mark.
  Whales

(Nature's children)
Includes indêx.
ISBN 0-7172-1897-X (bound) — ISBN 0-7172-2756-1 (pbk.)

1. Whales—Juvenile literature.
I. Title.   II. Series.

QL737.C4S5   1984   j599.5   C84-099568-7

Paperback:
Cover design: Tania Craan
Cover photo: The Stock market
                    Inc.

Casebound:
Cover Photo: Bora Merdsoy/
                    Image Index

What animal is bigger than any other animal on Earth, but has no teeth? If you guessed the Blue Whale, congratulations! The mighty Blue can grow to weigh as much as 21 African elephants. That is bigger than any dinosaur ever was.

Have you ever heard someone talking about having "a whale of a time"? That usually means that the person had a lot of fun, or a lot of trouble, or a lot of something-or-other. When you think of a whale, you think of something big, so it is not surprising that people sometimes use the word whale when they mean a LOT of something.

Yet not all whales are big. Did you know that some whales, such as the dolphin and the porpoise, are no bigger than a person? There are probably a lot of things about whales that will surprise you.

Long-distance traveler. (Gray Whale)

Not a Big Fish

Are whales big fish? No! There is one very big difference between fish and whales; whales are mammals, just like dogs, or cats or even you.

Because whales live in the sea, they are called marine mammals.

Mammals are animals that have lungs and breathe air. Just as you must swim up to the surface for a gulp of air after an underwater dive, so too do whales. They swim up to the surface from time to time and take in air through a blowhole. Fish do not need to do this. Instead they take the oxygen they need

Lungs extract oxygen from air taken in through blowhole.

Whiskers at some stage in life.

Young born alive.

Horizontal tail fin moves up and down.

WHALE

right from the water through their gills.

Mammals are warm blooded. That means that no matter how cold it is, their body temperature stays much the same. And mammals, including whales, are born alive and take milk from their mother.

Finally, all mammals have hair, at least during one stage of their life. With marine mammals, the hair appears only as whiskers. All whales are born with whiskers, and some keep them all their lives. With most whales, however, the whiskers fall off a few days after they are born.

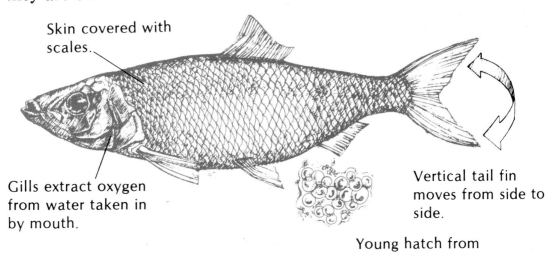

Skin covered with scales.

Gills extract oxygen from water taken in by mouth.

Vertical tail fin moves from side to side.

Young hatch from eggs.

FISH

Once Upon a Time, Long Ago . . .

Scientists believe that some 70 million years ago whales lived on land and looked very different. Why did they become water animals?

Perhaps food ran out on land, and the hungry whales went into the sea looking for food. Perhaps they stayed in the water to keep away from land enemies. Little by little, over many many generations, their bodies changed so that living in the sea would be easier. For instance, whales now have flippers instead of hands and feet like yours. But a whale's flippers have bones very much like those found in human hands. It seems likely that when whales lived on land, they had hands. As time passed, their hands slowly became flippers so that they could swim better. This is just one of many changes the land whales may have gone through to become sea whales.

Whales were probably smaller when they lived on land. Only animals living in water can grow as big as some whales do because the water supports their body weight.

A Whale of a Family

Whales are not only big in size, they also belong to a big family. There are over ninety different kinds of whales—from the small porpoise to the giant Blue Whale.

There are two main types of whales in this whale of a family: whales with teeth and whales without teeth. These two types of whales eat different foods and catch their food in different ways. They are also different in size. In general, the big whales are toothless whales. As well, a male toothed whale is larger than a female, but in the toothless group, the female is usually bigger than the male.

Overleaf:

The Finback Whale is named for its large dorsal fin.

Human Hand

Whale flipper.

Notice the similarity between the bones in the whale's flipper and those in a human hand.

Whales with Teeth

Toothed whales can be small like the dolphin and porpoise, or quite big, like the Sperm Whale.

Small or big, however, toothed whales are dainty eaters—they eat one fish at a time, swallowing it whole. They use their teeth for catching hold of their food, not chewing it.

Toothed whales eat mostly small fish and squid. Some use suction to suck food up from the ocean floor, much as a vacuum cleaner sucks up dirt and crumbs. Most often, toothed whales are seen traveling and hunting in groups called schools or herds. Sometimes hundreds of whales travel together in one herd and they work together to corral or trap fast-moving fish. When fishermen see these herds of whales, they know that lots of fish must be nearby.

Some toothed whales have more than 200 teeth, but the Narwhal (sometimes called the Unicorn Whale) usually has only one.

The Toothless Whales

The whales without teeth are called baleen
whales. Instead of teeth, they have as many as
400 plates called baleen hanging down from
the roof of their mouth. They use the baleen
to filter food out of the water. How?

Baleen whales are gulpers. They swim with
their mouths open taking in tonnes of water
full of plankton and tiny fish. Then, they close
their mouths and drain the water back out
through the baleen. The plankton and fish
cannot get through and are trapped in the
baleen. Then the whale's mighty tongue scoops
up the food and the whale swallows it.

Baleen whales are called the great whales
because they are so big. Even the smallest of
the great whales, the Minke, is about as long
as two cars! Would you have guessed that
animals that eat such tiny bits of food could
grow to be the biggest animals on Earth? Of
course, they eat huge amounts. A Blue Whale
may well eat 4000 kilograms (9000 pounds) in
one day.

Opposite page:

*Despite their large
size whales are
very streamlined
and move through
the water with
ease.*

The Better Not to See You

If you could look down at a whale in the water, the dark color on its back would blend in with the darker water below. If you were underwater and a whale swam above you, its light underside would blend in with the light from above. This type of coloring—dark top and light underside—is called counter-shading. It makes it harder for the whale's enemies and prey to see it in the water.

Baleen whales' bodies are usually light gray to brown or black on top with a lighter underside. Toothed whales range in color from the pure white Beluga Whale to the coal black Pilot Whale, but most of them, too, are gray with a lighter underside.

Since the Beluga is the only pure white whale in the world it is often called the White Whale. In fact, Beluga means "white one" in Russian.

Coming Up for Air

A whale cannot breathe through its mouth as you can. It gets air by breathing through an opening on the top of its head called a blowhole. This blowhole acts like a kind of nose. And because it is at the top of its head, a whale can breathe without having to stick its whole head out of the water.

As the whale's head comes to the surface of the water and into the air, the nostrils in its blowhole open and let out the used air in a "cough." The whooshing sound of the air being let out can be heard a long way away. Then new air is taken in, the nostrils shut and the whale's head slides under the water surface again. Each breath takes only one or two seconds.

A whale would drown if it did not come to the surface for air from time to time. Because of this, whales are not able to sleep for long periods of time. Instead they take short "cat naps" many times a day.

Spotting a Spout

When a whale lets its breath out through its blowhole, you can see it—it looks like a spout of water spray.

It is hard to get close to a whale, but you can often tell one type from another by its spout. The Gray Whale has a short bushy spout. The Sperm Whale shoots out its air on an angle. The Blue Whale has a tall skinny spout. And the Right Whale's spout is shaped like a heart!

A whale's spout is not composed of water as you might think. It is air that becomes visible when the water vapor in it condenses—just as your breath does on a cold day.

Sights and Sounds

What is it like when you open your eyes underwater? Does everything look blurry? For a whale, it is just the opposite. Whales can see very well under the water, but above the surface, in air, they cannot see well at all!

However, even under water, whales cannot see far; it is often too dark and murky. Whales therefore depend a lot on their keen sense of hearing. Sound travels faster in water than in air, so whales can hear sounds quickly and often from a long way off.

Toothed whales can even "see" with sound. They make a clicking noise that sounds rather like a rusty door being opened and closed. Then they wait for the echo of these clicks to bounce off an object and come back. The time between sending and receiving the clicks tells the whale how far away an object is. The whale can also tell the object's size, shape and the direction in which it is moving.

This process is called echolocation. Scientists have shown how it works by placing small rubber cups over a dolphin's eyes so it could not see. Then they sent the dolphin out to swim through a maze of hoops, and it did it perfectly every time!

Coming to Their Senses

Since whales spend so little time in air, they seem to have lost the sense of smell. (It is not possible to smell things under water.) Instead they have a well-developed sense of taste. Whales in oceanariums are so sensitive to tastes that they will refuse food if it has gone slightly bad.

The whale sends out a series of clicking sounds, sometimes as many as 400 per second. When the sounds reach an object they bounce off and echo back. The timing of the returning clicks tells the whale a great deal about the nature and location of the object.

Echolocation

Super Swimmers and Deep Divers

Whales are expert swimmers. They glide through the water by moving their tail fluke up and down. The fluke is very strong, and some whales can swim very fast. The paddle-like pectoral flippers—the "arms" on either side of a whale's body—are sometimes used when turning. The dorsal fin found on the back of most whales helps them to keep steady in the water.

Whales can make long, deep dives into the ocean. To help them do this, they can slow down their heartbeat, so that their air supply lasts longer. During a dive, blood only goes to the most important parts of the whale's body—the brain, heart and lungs. Also, a whale's blood carries more oxygen than that of most other animals.

Toothed whales are good divers because they must often dive deep to catch their food. Baleen whales usually dive down only to about 150 metres (500 feet). They will take a few short, shallow dives, then one long dive that may last for half an hour.

Opposite page:

Notice the barnacles on this Humpback Whale's head. A single whale may have as much as half a tonne of barnacles attached to it!

Nature's Loudest Songs

Whales can make a great variety of sounds including screams, squeaks and moans. But perhaps the whale most famous for its voice is the Humpback.

Humpback Whales are known for their singing. Their songs are among the longest and loudest songs heard in nature. Some may last for 30 minutes and can be heard over a long distance. Scientists are still not sure exactly how whales make these sounds or what they mean. Are they a greeting call? A call for help? Or are they similar to the bark or growl of a dog?

Some people believe the sounds are the way that whales talk to each other. Land animals leave tracks or a scent to send messages to others of their kind. Whales cannot do this, so maybe their underwater sounds are a way to keep in touch with each other.

Humpback Whales.

The Long Journey

A whale may travel thousands of kilometres each year. Some whales roam the oceans freely, but most travel within a certain large area—feeding in one place, mating and giving birth in another. Whales usually feed in cold northern waters and swim to warm southern waters to have their babies. This journey is called migration.

One baleen whale, the Gray Whale, has the longest migration of any mammal in the world. Each year, some of these whales spend summers off the coast of Alaska, then they travel south and spend the winter off the coast of Mexico. Sometimes the journey south will take as long as three months.

Species of whales most commonly found in North American waters (illustration overleaf)

Beluga Whale. A toothed whale that is pure white when fully grown. Found mainly in shallow Arctic waters.

Blue Whale. A baleen whale that weighs about 80 000 kilograms (180 000 pounds). The largest of all whales.

Bottlenose Dolphin. A small toothed whale usually found in warmer waters. The star of most oceanarium shows.

Bowhead Whale. A large baleen whale whose baleen is about 4 metres (14 feet) long, the longest of any whale.

Fin Whale. The fastest swimmer of the baleen whales, going 30 kilometres (20 miles) per hour. Prefers deep waters.

Gray Whale. Fairly large baleen whale that spends a lot of time near shore. In recent years some have become quite friendly.

Humpback Whale. A baleen whale that has very large flippers, up to 5 metres (16 feet) in length. The most active of the baleen whales.

Killer Whale. A toothed whale that grows to about 9 metres (30 feet). It is known for its intelligence—and for its big appetite.

Narwhal A toothed whale, the male of which (and very occasionally the female) has an external tusk that may reach a length of 3 metres (10 feet).

Minke Whale. The smallest of the baleen whales, the Minke seems to eat fish more often than any other baleen whale.

Right Whale. In early whaling days this baleen whale was considered the ''right'' one to hunt because it is such a slow swimmer.

Sperm Whale. The largest of the toothed whales and the deepest diver in the ocean. May dive more than 2 kilometres (3 miles) down.

KILLER WHALES

FIN WHALE

BELUGA

BOWHEAD

GRAY WHALE

BOTTLENOSE DOLPHINS

SPERM WHALE

HUMPBACK

MINKE WHALES

NARWHAL

.UE WHALE

RIGHT WHALE

Blanket of Blubber

Gray Whales and some other kinds of whales spend the summer months in the cold waters of the north because there is lots of food there. The whales eat huge amounts and store some of what they eat as fat in a thick layer of blubber. The Bowhead Whale, for example, has blubber that is more than half a metre (2 feet) thick! This layer of blubber acts like a thick winter coat. It helps to keep a whale warm by keeping in its body heat and keeping out the cold.

In the early winter, when ice begins to form over the water and there is not as much food, the whales begin to swim south. During their journey they do not stop to eat or even to rest.

Some whales, such as the Beluga and Narwhal, stay in the colder waters all year round. In the winter, when food is scarce, they absorb the stored fat in their blubber to give them energy.

Beluga Whale.

All in the Family

Most whales are ready to mate when they are about six years old. Mating whales play together and have been seen jumping and splashing about with each other. They gently nuzzle and "sing" to each other as they press their giant bodies together. Sometimes two males will fight over a female.

Whales are choosy about a mate, and once they have chosen, they are very affectionate. They splash in the water together, roll together and hug each other with their flippers. Some types of whales may even stay together for life.

No one is sure why whales breach, but it may be just for the fun of it!

A Warm Water Cradle

Females usually give birth to one baby, called a calf, every two or three years. Since a baby whale does not have a layer of blubber to keep it warm, it is best if it is born in warm water.

Some whale babies, such as those of the Gray Whale and the Humpback, are born in warm lagoons and shallow inlets. There they are safe from the cold, crashing waves of the ocean and safe from enemies, such as sharks and Killer Whales.

Narwhals and other whales that do not migrate to warmer waters simply move closer to the shore during the arctic summer to have their calves.

A baby whale can keep up with its fast-swimming mom by keeping close to her side. The water passing between their two bodies actually pulls the calf along.

A Big Beautiful Baby

A baby whale is huge! A newborn Blue Whale, for example, may weigh 2000 kilograms (4400 pounds) and be as long as two cars.

Although baby whales are born under water, they do not stay there long. They cannot breathe under water. As soon as her baby is born, the mother quickly helps it get to the surface for its first breath of air. She does this by pushing it up with her snout and guiding it with her flippers. Other female whales may help her.

A newborn whale is a very hungry baby! Just like a human baby, the newborn calf gets milk from its mother. It nuzzles close to her and nurses on her milk. A big baby Blue Whale can drink what would amount to almost 600 cartons of milk in one day! The milk is very rich, and the calf grows quickly.

The baby whale stays close to its mother, swimming under her flippers. A mother whale will do anything to keep her baby from being hurt. If danger is near, a mother whale can become quite fierce.

Opposite page:

Beluga Whales are not born white. It will take about five years before this calf takes on the complete coloring of its parents.

Whale School

One of the first things a mother whale teaches her baby is when to come up for air. The calf learns by imitating its mother's every movement. They swim, surface, breathe and then dive together. Soon the calf has learned what to do, and it is ready to enter the rougher waters of the open ocean.

Unlike a human baby who is completely helpless at birth, a newborn whale is well prepared for life in the ocean. But it still needs the lessons from its mother to improve its skills at surfacing, breathing, swimming and diving.

A baleen calf will nurse from its mother for six to eight months. Calves of toothed whales usually nurse longer—up to two years. They need the longer nursing period because they have more to learn about hunting and catching food than the baleen whales. Toothed whale calves generally stay close to their mother until she becomes pregnant again. After that, the young whale is pretty much on its own, although it will stay with the herd.

A whale of a tail!

There are several places in North America, including the coasts of British Columbia and California, the Gulf of St. Lawrence and the Bay of Fundy, where whales come close enough to shore for people to watch them.

A Whale of a Time

Most whales are playful animals. They spend
hours diving and splashing about. They leap
high into the air, then come crashing down on
their side with a big splash. This is called
breaching. Whales seem to enjoy each other
and are curious about the world around them.

Many people find it interesting to watch
schools of whales in the water. Every year
when thousands of Gray Whales migrate to the
warm lagoons off the coast of Mexico, whale
watchers go out in small boats to look at
them. Some of the whales have become very
friendly and let the people get close enough to
pet them. They may even push a small boat
around with their snout or come up under it
and lift it gently with their back. All of this is
in fun and everyone has a whale of a time!
The whales seem to enjoy the whale watchers
as much as the whale watchers enjoy them!

Gentle Giants

Whales seem to be very caring animals, and there have been many stories of whales helping each other. Some people once saw two adult Gray Whales helping a baby whale that was stuck on a sandbar. The calf was struggling around on the land and crying out. The two adults jumped out of the water, as if looking for the baby. When they spotted it, they swam over and slid up on the sandbar. With one whale on either side of the baby, they rocked until the calf was tightly sandwiched between them. Then they rocked together until they all slid off the sandbar into the water.

Opposite page:

What lies in the minds of these intelligent animals? No one knows for sure, but scientists hope that someday we will be able to communicate with them.

The Long Trip Back

Many whales stay in the warm breeding waters until spring. Then they are ready to travel to their summer feeding grounds in the north where the food supply is much greater. The new mothers and babies are the last to begin the long journey. This gives the calves extra time to grow and become stronger for the swim north.

Learning about Whales

By studying whales in captivity, scientists have discovered much of what we know about these giants of the sea. But there are still many mysteries about whales for us to uncover.

For thousands of years, people have marveled at the great whales in the sea and wondered how they lived in the wild. Recently, with better underwater equipment, we have been able to study some whales more closely. We know more about whales than we ever have before. Still, the more we learn about them, the more we are fascinated by their intelligence, gentleness and their mastery of their watery world.

Words to Know

Baleen   Plates in the upper jaw of some whales that strain out the small animals the whale eats.

Blowhole   Nostril at the top of the whale's head through which it breathes (some whales have two blowholes).

Blubber   A layer of fat under the skin of most marine mammals.

Breaching   The act of a whale leaping out of the water.

Breed   To come together to produce young.

Counter-shading   The coloring of a whale that helps to make it less noticeable.

Echolocation   Method used by some whales to find their way under water by sending out sounds and listening to the returning echoes.

Fluke   Whale's tail fin.

Mammal   Any animal that breathes air, is warm blooded, gives birth to live young, lives on mother's milk when young, and has some kind of hair during some stage of its life.

Migration   To travel from one region or climate to another for feeding or breeding.

Plankton   Small animals and plants that live in the sea.

INDEX

Photo Credits: Pat Morrow (First Light Associated Photographers), page 4; Barrett and MacKay (Masterfile), pages 10-11; Janet Foster (Masterfile), page 12; Bora Merdsoy (Image Index), pages 15, 41, 42; Fred Bruemmer, pages 16, 38; R. Galbraith (Valan Photos), pages 19, 27, 45; Esther Schmidt (Valan Photos), page 20; Don Morton (FPG, Miller Services), page 24; T. Gregg Eligh (Miller Services), page 33; Bill Brooks (Master File), page 34; John Foster (Master File), page 37.

All art illustrations: Jenniffer Julich and Jeannette McNaughton

Printed and Bound in Italy by Lego SpA